TOP 10

Gaming

A FIREFLY BOOK

Published by Firefly Books Ltd. 2015

Copyright © 2015 Octopus Publishing Group Ltd

First printing

Publisher Cataloging-in-Publication Data (U.S.)

Terry, Paul, 1978-
    Top 10 for kids : gaming / Paul Terry.
[96] pages : color illustrations ; cm.
Summary: "A fact-book of the most popular video games and their best
features and characters" - Provided by publisher.
ISBN-13: 978-1-77085-564-9 (pbk.)
1. Video games - Juvenile literature. I. Title. II. Top ten for kids : gaming.
794.8 dc23   GV1469.3T4779 2015

Library and Archives Canada Cataloguing in Publication

Terry, Paul, 1978-, author
    Top 10 for kids : gaming / Paul Terry.
ISBN 978-1-77085-564-9 (pbk.)
    1. Video games-Miscellanea-Juvenile literature. I. Title. II. Title:
Top ten for kids.
GV1469.3.T47 2015   j794.8   C2015-902939-2

Published in the United States by
Firefly Books (U.S.) Inc.
P.O. Box 1338, Ellicott Station
Buffalo, New York 14205

Published in Canada by
Firefly Books Ltd.
50 Staples Avenue, Unit 1
Richmond Hill, Ontario L4B 0A7

Printed in China

First published in Great Britain in 2015 by Ticktock,
an imprint of Octopus Publishing Group Ltd
Carmelite House
50 Victoria Embankment
London, EC4V 0DZ
Written by: Paul Terry. Paul Terry asserts the moral
right to be identified as the author of this work.
Series Editor/Project Editor: Anna Bowles
Managing Editor: Karen Rigden
Creative Director: Miranda Snow
Production: Meskerem Berhane

TOP 10

PARENTS KEEP OUT!

Gaming

Paul Terry

FIREFLY BOOKS

TOP 10

PARENTS KEEP OUT!

Gaming

What's your favorite game? Who's your favorite character? What's the coolest console? You've got your list of the best, but do your friends agree, or is it PlayStation vs Xbox in a battle to the death? This book gives you the lowdown on what's hottest and most popular, courtesy of gamers Team T-10. Check out the sections on conventions and collectors' editions, too.

CONTENTS

MEET...
TEAM T-10

Before you dive into this fact-packed adventure, say hello to the super team who are ready and waiting to guide you through the amazing info zones.

MAY-TRIX

T-10 FILE

This technology-loving 10-year-old girl is the eldest of Team T-10. May-Trix has hundreds of gadgets and gizmos that she uses to scan her surroundings for exciting data. From analyzing animals' sizes and special abilities, to understanding robotics and space exploration, May-Trix adores it all.

APOLLO

T-10 FILE

There are the *Guardians of the Galaxy*, then there's the Keeper of the Comics... And that's Apollo! This 8-year-old boy is an amazing comic book artist, and knows everything there is to know about superheroes, movies, computer games, TV shows and cartoons. He's into sports and outer space, too.

SHAUN VERT

When it comes to extreme sports, fast vehicles, computer games and slammin' metal and rock music, 9-year-old Shaun is your guy! He doesn't go anywhere without his headphones, and he loves cool buildings (he designs skate parks, too). His cybernetic artificial arm allows him to do gravity-defying skateboard tricks.

Quantum is a very special 7-year-old. Her best friend is her cyborg fish Cy-Go, and her quantum-powered goldfish bowl means she can travel through time and space to learn about the past, the future and the furthest reaches of the universe! This pair love to relax with a movie as well.

QUANTUM

ZONE 1

The Biggest Games!

From home consoles to handheld wonders, these are the games that rule them all!

TOP 10 Biggest Selling Console Games Of All Time!

From the 1972 Magnavox Odyssey (the first ever home console) to the latest cutting-edge PS4, millions of consoles have been sold over the years. Which games are we playing on them?

	GAME	GENRE	RELEASED	PLATFORM	UNIT SALES (MILLIONS)
1	Wii Sports	Sports	2006	Wii	82.13
2	Super Mario Bros.	Platform	1985	NES*	40.24
3	Mario Kart Wii	Racing	2008	Wii	34.67
4	Wii Sports Resort	Sports	2009	Wii	32.45
5	Pokémon Red/Blue/Green	RPG	1996	Game Boy	31.37
6	Tetris	Puzzle	1989	Game Boy	30.26
7	New Super Mario Bros.	Platform	2006	DS	29.52
8	Wii Play	Party	2006	Wii	28.83
9	Duck Hunt	Shooter	1984	NES*	28.31
10	New Super Mario Bros. Wii	Platform	2009	Wii	27.55

Source: VGChartz   *Nintendo Entertainment System

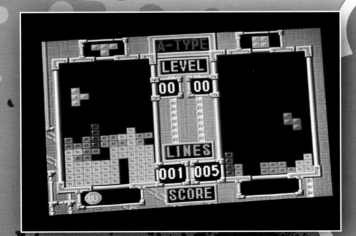

TETRIS

Since this massively popular puzzle (designed by Russian Alexey Pajitnov) first appeared in 1984 on the NES, there have been over 60 official versions made.

WII SPORTS

Wii Sports was the first ever Wii game, launched with the Nintendo console on Nov. 19, 2006. It has won multiple awards, including Best Sports Game at the 2006 Game Critics Awards.

Super Mario Bros.

The star of 192 video games, Mario is Nintendo's most successful franchise, selling more than 530 million games worldwide! Created by Japanese game designer and producer Shigeru Miyamoto, Mario and his heroic brother Luigi have battled various villains together since the 1983 arcade game Mario Bros.

the lowdown...

TEAM T-10 LOVES NEW SUPER MARIO BROS. WII BECAUSE ALL FOUR OF US CAN PLAY IT TOGETHER ON THE SAME SCREEN!

the lowdown...

LEGO City Undercover

A lot of *LEGO City Undercover*'s popularity comes from its "sandbox" roaming style: you can explore the city and put disguises on lead character Chase McCain to access different locations.

GAME ZONE

Team T-10 loves *Pikmin 3* because the aliens' color relates to their special power – like how the red ones cannot be hurt by fire.

12

TOP 10 Biggest Selling Wii U Games

Since its 2012 release, the touchscreen gamepad wonder that is the Wii U has won the hearts of gamers worldwide. These are the games that Wii U-sers love to play the most.

	GAME			GENRE	RELEASED	UNIT SALES (MILLIONS)
1	New Super Mario Bros. U			Action	2012	4.25
2	Nintendo Land		Action	2012	3.14	
3	Mario Kart 8		Racing	2014	2.80	
4	Super Mario 3D World		Platform	2013	2.31	
5	New Super Luigi U		Platform	2013	1.75	
6	Wii Party U		Party	2013	1.36	
7	The Legend of Zelda: The Wind Waker		Action	2013	1.07	
8	Pikmin 3		Strategy	2013	0.82	
9	LEGO City Undercover		Action	2013	0.81	
10	Donkey Kong Country: Tropical Freeze		Platform	2014	0.71	

Source: VGChartz

NEW SUPER LUIGI U CELEBRATED 30 YEARS OF THE CHARACTER AND 2013 WAS NAMED AS THE YEAR OF LUIGI.

NINTENDO LAND

Launched with the Wii U on Nov. 18, 2012, *Nintendo Land*'s 12 mini-games feature all the best Nintendo characters, including Link, Mario, Metroid, Yoshi and Donkey Kong.

TOP 10 Biggest Selling Wii Games

Even though Nintendo stopped building Wii units on Oct. 20, 2013, gamers are still Wii-ing in their millions.

	GAME	GENRE	RELEASED	UNIT SALES (MILLIONS)
1	Wii Sports	Sports	2006	82.13
2	Mario Kart Wii	Racing	2008	34.67
3	Wii Sports Resort	Sports	2009	32.45
4	Wii Play	Party	2006	28.83
5	New Super Mario Bros. Wii	Platform	2009	27.55
6	Wii Fit	Sports	2007	22.69
7	Wii Fit Plus	Sports	2009	21.53
8	Super Smash Bros. Brawl	Combat	2008	12.30
9	Super Mario Galaxy	Platform	2007	11.11
10	Just Dance 3	Party	2011	9.96

Source: VGChartz

Wii Sports

Released in-pack with the Wii console in November 2006, *Wii Sports* is not just the bestselling Wii game, it also reigns as the bestselling (PEGI 12 and under-rated) console game of all time!

Mario Kart Wii

Super Mario Kart roared into action on the SNES (Super Nintendo Entertainment System) in 1992. Twenty-two years and 10 games later, the franchise has made over $101 million. *Mario Kart 8* was released for the Wii U on May 29, 2014.

the **lowdown**...

TEAM T-10 REPORT

Party On!

Team T-10 likes to party... And we love the Wii's huge range of party games! Playing tennis and bowling with the motion-sensor controllers is our favorite way to spend a rainy day, even eight years after the Wii-mote first came out.

GAME ZONE

Just Dance 3 was awarded Favorite Video Game at the 2012 Nickelodeon Kids' Choice Awards.

TOP 10

Biggest selling PS3 Games

Take a quick look at this list. It's clear to see that PS3 owners love the thrill of fast-paced sports games more than any other kind.

← the **lowdown...**

FIFA SOCCER 13

- Released across 12 platforms between 2012-13, *FIFA 13* was the 20th in the game series. Its soundtrack of no less than 50 songs included tracks by Band of Horses and deadmau5.

THE MUSIC OF GT5 RANGES FROM MY CHEMICAL ROMANCE TO TCHAIKOVSKY!

GAME ZONE

LittleBigPlanet 2 just missed out on joining its predecessor in this Top 10 with global sales of 3.2 million.

	GAME	GENRE	RELEASED	UNIT SALES (MILLIONS)
1	**Gran Turismo 5**	**Racing**	**2010**	**10.46**
2	FIFA Soccer 13	Sports	2012	8.06
3	FIFA Soccer 14	Sports	2013	6.70
4	FIFA Soccer 12	Sports	2011	6.58
5	LittleBigPlanet	Platform	2008	5.52
6	FIFA Soccer 11	Sports	2010	5.03
7	Gran Turismo 5 Prologue	Racing	2007	4.17
8	Street Fighter IV	Combat	2009	3.98
9	MotorStorm	Racing	2006	3.83
10	Sports Champions	Sports	2010	3.69

Source: VGChartz

GRAN TURISMO 5

GT5 really stepped things up, with 16 players able to compete together online! The ever-popular night racing option made a comeback too. With 71 different race tracks and 26 locations to choose from, no wonder it won Best Racing Game at the 2011 Golden Joystick Awards. Fast, furious and fun!

ENDLESS ENGINES
In *Gran Turismo 5* you can choose from 1,000 different cars!

TOP 10 Biggest Selling PS4 Games

PS4 owners must be dedicated sports fans - a massive seven of these bestsellers involve goal-scoring, slam-dunking and touchdowns!

	GAME	GENRE	RELEASED	UNIT SALES (MILLIONS)
1	FIFA 15	Sports	2014	3.33
2	FIFA Soccer 14	Sports	2013	2.58
3	Knack	Action	2013	1.20
4	Need for Speed Rivals	Racing	2013	1.10
5	NBA 2K14	Sports	2013	1.04
6	Madden NFL 15	Sports	2014	0.95
7	Madden NFL 25	Sports	2013	0.69
8	LEGO Marvel Super Heroes	Action	2013	0.61
9	NBA 2K15	Sports	2014	0.57
10	EA Sports UFC	Sports	2014	0.54

Source: VGChartz

Madden NFL 15

EA Sports lets fans vote for the cover star via sports channel ESPN. Seattle Seahawks' cornerback Richard Sherman won the public vote. An amazing 30 Madden games have been released, selling more than 108 million copies!

IN 1988, JOHN MADDEN FOOTBALL WAS RELEASED, THE FIRST OF THE FRANCHISE.

ZONE 1: The Biggest Games!

GAME ZONE

Lego Marvel Super Heroes is one of 55 official LEGO video games made since 1997's LEGO Island.

A WHOPPING 155 PLAYABLE CHARACTERS IN LEGO MARVEL SUPER HEROES?! BRING IT ON!

the lowdown...

FIFA 2015

Released across 11 platforms (including iOS, Android and Windows smart phone devices), FIFA 15 included, for the first time, all 20 official Premier League stadiums.

MISSIONS POSSIBLE!

There are 11 extra bonus missions, one featuring S.H.I.E.L.D.'s Agent Coulson.

TOP 10 Biggest Selling Xbox One Games

It's one of the most powerful video game systems in the world today, and the number one game in this Top 10 is managing to race ahead of all the others.

	GAME	GENRE	RELEASED	UNIT SALES (MILLIONS)
1	Forza Motorsport 5	Racing	2013	1.55
2	FIFA Soccer 14	Sports	2013	1.02
3	FIFA 15	Sports	2014	0.90
4	Madden NFL 15	Sports	2014	0.71
5	NBA 2K14	Sports	2013	0.67
6	Madden NFL 25	Sports	2013	0.58
7	Need for Speed Rivals	Racing	2013	0.40
8	LEGO Marvel Super Heroes	Action	2013	0.38
9	Forza Horizon 2	Action	2014	0.37
10	NBA 2K15	Sports	2014	0.29

Source: VGChartz

GAME ZONE

PS4 and Xbox One gamers can scan their faces when creating an NBA 2K15 player!

Need For Speed Rivals

The *Need For Speed* franchise is over 20 years old. Its 1994 debut featured only seven tracks, but now gaming doesn't get much faster than this. *Rivals* is an open world environment with over 100 miles (160 km) to explore. You can play the story through as either a street racer or a police officer in hot pursuit.

NEED MOVIE CARS

You can download a Movie Pack with the *Need for Speed* movie's vehicles.

NEED FOR SPEED RIVALS' SOUNDTRACK FEATURES DOZENS OF BANDS, SUCH AS LINKIN PARK.

TEAM T-10 REPORT

SMALL TO BIG SCREEN!

On Mar. 12, 2014, the *Need For Speed* franchise exploded into cinemas for the first time. Aaron Paul starred as Tobey Marshall, a racer out to avenge the death of his best friend. It took over $203 million at the box office worldwide.

TOP 10 Biggest Selling PS Vita Games

Here's a gaming tongue-twister for you: this portable PlayStation proves most popular with players of platform games!

	GAME	GENRE	RELEASED	UNIT SALES (MILLIONS)
1	**LittleBigPlanet** PS Vita	**Platform**	**2012**	**0.84**
2	Need For Speed: Most Wanted	Racing	2012	0.74
3	Final Fantasy X / X-2 HD Remaster	RPG	2013	0.55
4	FIFA Soccer 12	Sports	2012	0.53
5	Rayman Origins	Platform	2012	0.50
6	Hot Shots Golf: World Invitational	Sports	2011	0.47
7	Gravity Rush	Action	2012	0.46
8	Tearaway	Action	2013	0.43
9	FIFA Soccer 13	Sports	2012	0.42
10	Virtual Tennis 4: World Tour	Sports	2011	0.40

Source: VGChartz

GRAVITY RUSH

Seen the movie *Gravity*? Wonder what it's like to change gravity? *Gravity Rush* let's you do that! The game uses traditional cel-shaded animation like the classic movie *Bambi*.

the lowdown...

LittleBigPlanet

In this, the fourth *LittleBigPlanet* game, the handheld PS Vita console added something extra special. You can touch the screen to interact with the environment that hero Sackboy wanders through!

NEED FOR SPEED: MOST WANTED

High-speed handheld racing doesn't get much better. Most of the cars available to use are secretly scattered, and Team T-10 loves finding new models and unlocking them to use.

WANT EVEN MORE NEED FOR SPEED: MOST WANTED THRILLS? DOWNLOADABLE EXTRA TERMINAL VELOCITY SPEEDS YOU INTO AN AIRPORT!

GAME ZONE

If you bought Need For Speed: Most Wanted on the PS3, you could use the Cross Buy feature and send a copy of the game to your PS Vita for free.

PlayStation

MY PET CY-GO AND I LOVE TIME TRAVEL. WE ADORE THE LITTLEBIGPLANET DOWNLOADABLE SACKBOY'S PREHISTORIC MOVES.

TOP 10 Biggest Selling Xbox 360 Games

There's nothing more exciting than playing your favorite sport on screen, and Xbox 360 owners clearly agree.

	GAME	GENRE	RELEASED	UNIT SALES (MILLIONS)
1	Kinect Adventures!	Party	2010	21.21
2	Kinect Sports	Sports	2010	5.89
3	Minecraft	Adventure	2013	5.58
4	Forza Motorsport 3	Racing	2009	5.42
5	FIFA Soccer 13	Sports	2012	5.09
6	Guitar Hero III: Legends of Rock	Party	2007	4.46
7	Forza Motorsport 4	Racing	2011	4.26
8	FIFA Soccer 12	Sports	2011	4.12
9	FIFA Soccer 14	Sports	2013	4.11
10	Forza Motorsport 2	Racing	2007	4.02

Source: VGChartz

Forza Motorsport 3

If you've got yourself the Ultimate Collection edition, you'll have an eye-popping 500 cars to choose from! Plus, they're all fully customizable. A total of 50 manufacturers officially licensed their vehicles to this 2009 game. If you can find the Limited Edition, you'll get a very rare Forza USB stick as well as five exclusive cars.

YOU CAN SPEED YOUR WAY THROUGH 200 EVENTS IN THE ONE-PLAYER CAMPAIGN.

I LOVE EXPLORING, AND KINECT ADVENTURES' MINI-GAME RIVER RUSH IS MY FAVORITE. YOU HAVE TO CAREFULLY JUMP AND STEP TO CONTROL YOUR RAFT AS IT ZOOMS DOWN WHITE WATER RAPIDS!

the lowdown...

Kinect Adventures!

This game uses the full-body motion sensor of the Xbox's Kinect camera system. Its mini-games involve jumping and bending your body and limbs. Team T-10 loves *20,000 Leaks*, where you stop water flowing in a "whack-a-mole" type game.

GAME ZONE

FIFA Soccer 12 made cash registers ring to the sum of $186 million in its first week on sale!

TOP 10 Biggest selling 3DS Games

Mario first appeared in *Donkey Kong* in 1981, and look at how many bestselling 3DS games he features in here...

the lowdown... →

SUPER MARIO 3D LAND

This souped-up Mario adventure makes the best use of the Nintendo 3DS' special screen. It has what is called an "autostereoscopic" screen. This means it gives the illusion that the player is looking at images with THREE dimensions, even though they're clearly looking at a two-dimensional display screen.

SUPER MARIO 3D LAND

GAME ZONE

Did you know that Luigi's Mansion: Dark Moon is a sequel that came 12 years later... Luigi's Mansion was released for the GameCube back in 2001.

	GAME	GENRE	RELEASED	UNIT SALES (MILLIONS)
1	Pokémon X/Y	RPG	2013	11.96
2	Mario Kart 7	Racing	2011	9.88
3	Super Mario 3D Land	Platform	2011	9.65
4	New Super Mario Bros. 2	Platform	2012	7.01
5	Animal Crossing: New Leaf	Action	2012	5.08
6	Luigi's Mansion: Dark Moon	Adventure	2013	3.81
7	Monster Hunter 4	RPG	2013	3.42
8	The Legend of Zelda: Ocarina of Time	Action	2011	3.41
9	Nintendogs + Cats	Simulation	2011	3.40
10	Super Smash Bros. for Wii and 3DS	Fighting	2014	3.10

Source: VGChartz

ANIMAL CROSSING: NEW LEAF

Enjoy life simulation games? This, the fourth in the franchise, has you play the town mayor. You live in a tent to begin with, but can progress to a house while you look after the town.

TEAM T-10 REPORT

TOURNAMENT TIME

Which of these games would be most popular with your friends? The T-10 team enjoys *Mario Kart 7*. Ask your friends and family which ones they would most like to challenge you to play.

ANIMAL CROSSING'S TOWN INCLUDES OWL-, TURTLE- AND HEDGEHOG-TYPE RESIDENTS.

TOP 10 Biggest Arcade Games

Back in the time before video games could be easily played at home, these 10 games sold more units to arcades than any others.

	GAME	RELEASED	UNIT SALES (MILLIONS)
1	**Pac-Man**	**1980**	**400,000**
2	Space Invaders	1978	360,000
3	Street Fighter II (all versions)	1991	200,000
4	Donkey Kong	1981	132,000
5	Ms. Pac-Man	1982	125,000
6	Asteroids	1979	100,000
7	Defender	1981	60,000
8	Centipede	1981	55,988
9	Galaxian	1979	40,000
10	Donkey Kong Jr.	1982	30,000

Source: VGChartz

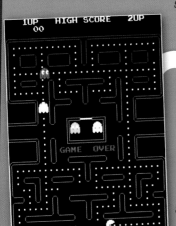

PAC-MAN
This legendary game has spawned over 30 spin-offs and sequels since its original 1980 arcade machine version. These include the classics *Ms. Pac-Man, Professor Pac-Man,* and even *Baby Pac-Man!*

Donkey Kong

Donkey Kong was created by Japanese games designer and producer Shigeru Miyamoto in 1981. It marks the first ever appearance of Mario, who dodges barrels thrown by the angry gorilla to save Pauline.

BEFORE GAMING WAS HANDHELD, GAMERS GATHERED AT COIN-OP GAMES (SHORT FOR "COIN-OPERATED").

the lowdown...

STREET FIGHTER II

The original Capcom arcade machine *Street Fighter* was released in 1987. This sequel entered arcades in 1991 and fast became the most famous fighting video game of all time. In its first four years, *Street Fighter II* took over $2 billion dollars!

TOP 10 Biggest Gaming Publishers

Two of the top three in this chart publish games and make their own consoles. Look how far ahead of the pack the number one is.

	PUBLISHER	NO. OF GAMES IN TOP 100 SELLERS
1	Nintendo	52
2	Activision	13
3	Sony Computer Entertainment	10
4	Take-Two Interactive	8
5	Microsoft Game Studios	5
=	Electronic Arts	5
7	Ubisoft	3
8	Bethesda Softworks	1
=	Red Orb	1
=	SquareSoft	1

Source: VGChartz

GAME ZONE

Activision's smash hit *Skylanders* series spun out of its *Spyro The Dragon* universe that began back in 1998 on the PlayStation.

ACTIVISION

This was the world's first ever independent developer and distributor of video games. Formed in 1979, one of their most popular games was 1982's *Pitfall*. These days, Activision is best known for *Skylanders, Guitar Hero* and *Tony Hawk's Pro Skater* series, to name a few.

the **lowdown**...

SONY COMPUTER ENTERTAINMENT

Set up in November 1993 when it launched Sony's PlayStation, the company now owns over 200 hit gaming franchises. These include fan favorites like *Gran Turismo*, *Buzz!*, *Ratchet & Clank* and *EyePet*. Its three main headquarters are based in Tokyo, Japan, London, England, and California.

THAT FAMOUS NINTENDO LETTERING AND LOGO? THEY HAVEN'T CHANGED IT SINCE THE 1970S.

TOP 10 Crazy Development Breakthroughs

Everything video gaming has become today is a result of amazing ideas and breakthroughs in technology. Which are your favorite devices and changes?

	TECHNOLOGY	COMPANY	BREAKTHROUGH
1	Periscope	Sega	1968 electro-mechanical arcade machine
2	PS3	Sony	First full HD console + Blu-ray player
3	Game & Watch	Nintendo	First handheld LCD gaming
4	Wii	Nintendo	Motion sensor board & controllers
5	Kinect	Microsoft	Full-body motion sensor game play
6	Game Boy	Nintendo	First global hit handheld console
7	Virtual Reality	Various	Interactive VR helmet and glove
8	PlayStation 2	Sony	First-ever CD-ROM based console
9	Amiga	Commodore	Advanced home computer gaming
10	Game Gear	Sega	First color handheld console

Source: VGChartz

PS3 Phenomenon!

Blu-ray launched in June 2006 and the PS3 took the risk of including a Blu-ray player when it launched a few months later in November. Thankfully Blu-ray has become a standard format for games, movies and TV shows!

VIRTUAL REALITY

The latest method of giving the gamer a "virtual reality" experience is with Oculus VR's Oculus Rift HMD (head-mounted display). After a prototype was shown at the E3 event in 2012 (in Los Angeles), Oculus VR raised finances (including $2.4 million via Kickstarter) to complete the device.

TEAM T-10 REPORT

YOUR MOVE!

All of these developments came from ideas... So Team T-10 have a challenge for YOU! What would you like to see as the next big breakthrough in video gaming? Your idea could become the next big thing!

Kinect

First developed for the Xbox 360 in 2010, its successor, the Xbox One, has a larger and more powerful Kinect camera. Kinect is the fastest-selling electronic device, shifting an amazing eight million units in the first two months of release.

the lowdown...

GAME ZONE

Twenty-two Kinect games have been made since 2010, totaling $37 million in takings!

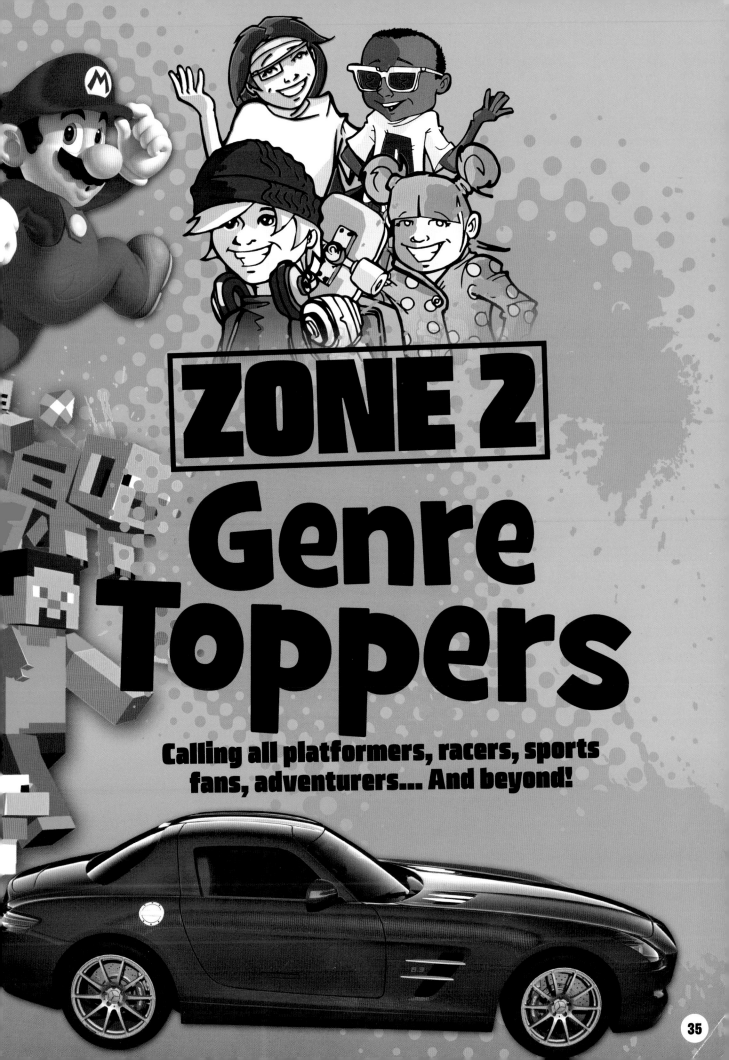

ZONE 2

Genre Toppers

Calling all platformers, racers, sports fans, adventurers... And beyond!

Racing

Are you a video game fan who loves the screech of wheels? You'll be pleased to know that nearly 3,000 racing games have been made! The top 100 best-selling racers have notched up 374.18 million sales.

the lowdown...

GAME ZONE

Tetris represent over 45 percent of the 66.97 million unit sales of the top 10 puzzlers.

TOP 10 Most Successful Genre Leader

Ask your friends which kind of video game they think is the most popular, and then stun them with these jaw-dropping unit sales.

	GENRE	GAME	RELEASED	PLATFORM	UNIT SALES (MILLIONS)
1	Sports	Wii Sports	2006	Wii	81.42
2	Platform	Super Mario Bros.	1985	NES	40.24
3	Racing	Mario Kart Wii	2008	Wii	33.84
4	RPG	Pokémon Red/Blue/Green	1996	Game Boy	31.37
5	Puzzle	Tetris	1989	Game Boy	30.26
6	Party	Wii Play	2006	Wii	28.74
7	Shooter	Duck Hunt	1984	NES	28.31
8	Simulation	Nintendogs	2005	DS	24.61
9	Fighting	Super Smash Bros. Brawl	2008	Wii	12.32
10	Adventure	Myst	1994	PC	8.03

Source: VGChartz

MARIO SERIES BAD GUY BOWSER IS KNOWN AS KOOPER IN JAPAN, HENCE "KOOPER TROOPERS"!

SUPER SMASH BROS. BRAWL

Fighting

Released Jan. 31, 2008, Super Smash Bros. Brawl is the eighth-most-successful Wii game ever. The first ever Super Smash Bros. title was released in 1999 on the Nintendo's N64 console.

TOP 10 Biggest Sports Games

With its motion-sensor controllers, it's no surprise that the Wii is the king of sports games. Which of these hit titles have you played?

	GAME	PLATFORM	RELEASED	UNIT SALES (MILLIONS)
1	Wii Sports	Wii	2006	82.16
2	Wii Sports Resort	Wii	2009	32.46
3	Wii Fit	Wii	2007	22.69
4	Wii Fit Plus	Wii	2009	21.54
5	Mario & Sonic at the Olympic Games	Wii	2007	7.94
6	FIFA Soccer 14	PS3	2013	6.72
7	Zumba Fitness	Wii	2010	6.60
8	FIFA Soccer 12	PS3	2011	6.59
9	Kinect Sports	Xbox 360	2010	5.90
10	Madden NFL 2004	PS2	2003	5.23

Source: VGChartz

GAME ZONE

None of the PS4's sports games made it into the top ten, but the console's ten biggest sports titles have racked up over 11 million sales.

I LOVE HOW THE MOTION SENSOR TECHNOLOGY LETS ME CHALLENGE MY TEAM T-10 BUDDIES TO BOXING, TABLE TENNIS, BOWLING, ATHLETICS, VOLLEYBALL AND SOCCER IN KINECT SPORTS.

FIFA 14

This, the 21st *FIFA* video game, gave players an even more realistic soccer experience. The special programing meant that the players reacted more emotionally to events on the field, like missed goals and tackles.

the **lowdown**...

Mario & Sonic at the Olympic Games

Rival gaming franchises for decades, this was the first official game to feature both Mario and Sonic and their fellow characters. It was also an official game for the Beijing 2008 Summer Olympics.

TOP 10 Biggest Platform Games

Leaping, bouncing, crawling, smashing. These games have it all, and power-ups galore! See which king of the platformers dominates this list.

	GAME	PLATFORM	RELEASED	UNIT SALES (MILLIONS)
1	Super Mario Bros.	NES	1985	40.24
2	New Super Mario Bros.	DS	2006	29.53
3	New Super Mario Bros. Wii	Wii	2009	27.53
4	Super Mario World	SNES	1990	20.61
5	Super Mario Land	Game Boy	1989	18.14
6	Super Mario Bros. 3	NES	1988	17.28
7	Super Mario 64	N64	1996	11.89
8	Super Mario Land 2: 6 Golden Coins	Game Boy	1992	11.18
9	Super Mario Galaxy	Wii	2007	11.12
10	Super Mario All-Stars	SNES	1993	10.55

Source: VGChartz

SUPER MARIO GALAXY

It wasn't just this game's 3D-style galactic adventuring that won it awards. The Platinum Edition of its soundtrack contains a massive 81 tracks across two discs.

SUPER MARIO ALL-STARS

This has four classic NES games (*Super Mario Bros. 1, 2* and *3* and *The Lost Levels*) spruced up for the SNES. It was also issued for the Wii in 2010.

GAME
ZONE

Across all consoles, over 3,300 different platform games have been made!

MARIO HAS EVEN STARRED IN EDUCATIONAL GAMES, LIKE THE HISTORY-BASED MARIO'S TIME MACHINE IN 1993.

the **lowdown**...

Super Mario Bros.

First came 1983's Mario Bros. Since 1985's Super Mario Bros., the franchise exploded in popularity. Over 200 Mario and Luigi games have been made, resulting in over 550 million unit sales. Entertainment website IGN called the original Super Mario Bros. "the greatest game of all time."

TOP 10 Biggest RPG Games

When it comes to RPGs (Role-Playing Games), there is clearly one franchise to rule them all... AND you've got to catch them all.

GAME ZONE

The year 2015 saw the release of an arcade machine game (and console versions) called *Pokkén* Tournament. Imagine a fighting franchise like *Street Fighter* or *Tekken* but with Pokémon creatures!

	GAME	PLATFORM	RELEASED	UNIT SALES (MILLIONS)
1	Pokémon Red/Blue/Green Version	Game Boy	1996	31.37
2	Pokémon Gold/Silver Version	Game Boy	1999	23.10
3	Pokémon Diamond/Pearl Version	Game Boy	2006	18.17
4	Pokémon Ruby/Sapphire Version	Game Boy	2002	15.85
5	Pokémon Black/White Version	Game Boy	2010	14.90
6	Pokémon Yellow: Special Pikachu Edition	Game Boy	1998	14.64
7	Pokémon X/Y	3DS	2013	12.02
8	Pokémon Heart Gold/Soul Silver Version	DS	2009	11.66
9	Pokémon FireRed/LeafGreen Version	GBA	2004	10.49
10	World of Warcraft	PC	2004	10.07

Source: VGChartz

> WHAT DID THE CHIKORITA SAY ON HALLOWEEN? CHIK-OR-TREET-A!!!

Pokémon Black/White Version

There have been 719 Pokémon creatures, and 87 *Pokémon* video games have been made across all platforms, selling almost 240 million units. There's even a black and white version.

the **lowdown**...

World Of Warcraft

Since its 2004 debut, the MMORPG (Massively Multiplayer Online Role-Playing Game) *World of Warcraft* series has sold over 20 million units. But its subscribers have made it $10 billion, making it the most profitable game ever.

Biggest Adventure Games

Exploring mystical lands and battling super-villains are just two elements of the greatest adventure video games of all time.

	GAME	PLATFORM	RELEASED	UNIT SALES (MILLIONS)
1	**Myst**	PC	**1994**	**8.03**
2	Minecraft	Xbox 360	**2013**	**5.70**
3	Professor Layton and the Curious Village	DS	**2007**	**5.14**
4	Zelda II: The Adventure of Link	NES	**1987**	**4.38**
5	Professor Layton and the Diabolical Box	DS	**2007**	**3.88**
6	Luigi's Mansion: Dark Moon	3DS	**2013**	**3.83**
7	LEGO Indiana Jones: The Original Adventures	Xbox 360	**2008**	**3.69**
8	Rugrats: Search for Reptar	PS	**1998**	**3.34**
9	LEGO Batman: The Videogame	Xbox 360	**2008**	**3.22**
10	Professor Layton and the Unwound Future	DS	**2008**	**3.19**

Source: VGChartz

LEGO Batman: The Videogame

The LEGO video game franchise has sold over 108 million units, and 18.7 million of those are *LEGO Batman* games. Since the first in 2008, the LEGO Dark Knight has featured on 13 gaming platforms.

the lowdown...

Minecraft

Since Swedish designer Markus Persson came up with *Minecraft* in 2009, the sandbox game has exploded in popularity. Over 54 million copies have been sold, and Microsoft bought Mojang for $2.5 billion!

YOU CAN EVEN BUY 10 DIFFERENT LEGO MINECRAFT TOY SETS!

GAME ZONE

MineCon is a fan convention dedicated to *Minecraft*. Over 7,500 people attend each year!

IF YOU OWN AN ADVENTURE GAME, YOU'RE PLAYING ONE OF THE 440 MILLION UNITS OF ADVENTURE TITLES THAT HAVE BEEN SOLD!

TOP 10 Biggest Racing Games

Start your engines! We've put all of the racing games against each other, and the 10 best sellers have blasted past the finishing lines with amazing sales...

MARIO KART 8 HAS ITS OWN WEBSITE: MARIOKART8.NINTENDO.COM

Mario Kart DS

Mario Kart DS also holds the title of being the third best-selling DS game of all time. There have been 10 *Mario Kart* titles released, totaling over 100 million sales.

the **lowdown...**

Gran Turismo 5

The *Gran Turismo* series has been screeching around hairpin bends since 1997! The franchise has clocked up 71 million sales, and *GT5* brought online playing to the brand for the first time. It also got the likes of NASCAR involved officially, with 1,000 cars to choose from.

	GAME	PLATFORM	RELEASED	UNIT SALES (MILLIONS)
1	Mario Kart Wii	Wii	2008	34.70
2	Mario Kart DS	DS	2005	22.97
3	Gran Turismo 3: A-Spec	PS2	2001	14.98
4	Gran Turismo 4	PS2	2004	11.66
5	Gran Turismo	PS	1997	10.95
6	Gran Turismo 5	PS3	2010	10.47
7	Mario Kart 7	3DS	2011	9.92
8	Mart Kart 64	N64	1996	9.87
9	Gran Turismo 2	PS	1999	9.49
10	Super Mario Kart	SNES	1992	8.76

Source: VGChartz

GAME ZONE

Producer of the *Gran Turismo* game series, Kazunori Yamauchi, and his work is the focus of the 2014 documentary *KAZ: Pushing the Virtual Divide.*

THE FIRST GRAN TURISMO GAME, WHICH CAME OUT IN 1997, TOOK FIVE YEARS TO MAKE!

ZONE 3
Characters & Worlds

Let's meet some of the best heroes and villains in the coolest realms...

TOP 10 Most Expensive Games To Develop

We often hear about movies costing hundreds of millions to make, but video games are just as expensive. Here are the 10 biggest bank-busters.

	GAME	TOTAL DEVELOPMENT + MARKETING COSTS (MILLIONS $)
1	Final Fantasy VII	145
2	Disney Infinity	100
3	Shenmue	93
4	Gran Turismo 5	80
5	Rift	70
6	World of Warcraft	60
7	DC Universe Online	50
=	Pokémon Red/Green/Blue	50
9	Wii Fit	40
=	Final Fantasy IX	40

Source: VGChartz

DCU ONLINE

DC Universe Online is a kind of game called an MMORPG. This stands for Massively Multiplayer Online Role-Playing Game. You can even create your own new superhero!

PS2 PATIENCE

The mega-selling 1997 *Final Fantasy* game for the PS2 game was the first in the popular franchise to have 3D graphics. However, the game was so complex that it took three YEARS to make!

DISNEY INFINITY

With 29 characters from 12 different Disney franchises released so far, it's no wonder this game is so popular. These include *Sorcerer's Apprentice*, featuring Mickey Mouse from the 1940 movie *Fantasia* and Anna and Elsa from 2013's *Frozen*.

THE INCREDIBLES ALSO HAVE THREE GAMES, INCLUDING *THE INCREDIBLES: RISE OF THE UNDERMINER*, A SEQUEL TO THE MOVIE.

NEED FOR SPEED

If you are a fan of racing games, then Team T-10 is sure you've heard of the Need for Speed franchise. But did you know that there having been a massive 116 releases bearing that phrase across all major platforms?

the lowdown...

GAME ZONE

MARIO vs. SONIC
During the 1990s, Sega's Sonic the Hedgehog and Nintendo's Super Mario were sworn sales enemies. However, since 2007, the duo have starred in three different Olympic games titles.

TETRIS

A massive 70 game releases have featured the addictive, shape-twisting challenges of *Tetris*. Its Game Boy version alone, from back in 1989, has sold more than 30 million copies.

TOP 10 Biggest Selling Game Brands

If you come up with a massively popular idea, that idea can become a brand that makes money over and over again...

	FRANCHISE	TOTAL UNIT SALES (MILLIONS)
1	Mario	531.87
2	Pokémon	235.74
3	Wii (incl. Wii Sports)	215.78
4	FIFA	137.84
5	Sonic the Hedgehog	108.18
6	LEGO	106.85
7	Final Fantasy	106.53
8	Need for Speed	94.41
9	Tetris	93.67
10	The Sims	92.89

Source: VGChartz

WII

Wii Sports was the first ever Wii game, launched with the Nintendo console on Nov. 19, 2006. It has won multiple awards, including Best Sports Game at the 2006 Game Critics' Awards.

QUANTUM AND I LOVE THE JURASSIC PARK FRANCHISE, BUT SADLY ITS 41 RELEASES ONLY AMOUNT TO 2.4 MILLION UNIT SALES, SO IT'S NOWHERE NEAR THE TOP 10.

Transformers

This game is the sequel to 2010's *Transformers: War for Cybertron.* Those Autobots and Decepticons are big business in the gaming world, with over 13 million sales!

the **lowdown**...

GAME ZONE

Do YOU have an idea for a video game? All of the ones you enjoy playing started off as an idea in someone's head, so let your imagination run wild and see what you can come up with!

TOP 10

Awesome Gaming Worlds

From battling alien robots to majestic, eye-popping landscapes, these games are a joy to look at.

1. **Ni No Kuni:** The Wrath of the White Witch
2. Journey
3. Skylanders: Giants
4. Ico
5. The Legend of Zelda: Ocarina of Time
6. Limbo
7. Transformers: Fall of Cybertron
8. Myst
9. Super Mario World
10. Animal Crossing: New Leaf

Source: VGChartz

NINO KUNI

This PS3 cult hit has sold 1.39 million copies. Animation sequences were created by the same amazing minds behind the Studio Ghibli anime movies like 2013's *The Wind Rises*.

DINOBOT GRIMLOCK MAKES AN APPEARANCE IN THE MOVIE TRANSFORMERS: AGE OF EXTINCTION.

TOP 10 Biggest Mario Games

Those plumber brothers truly have taken over the platform gaming world! Check out their game sales...

	NAME	GENRE	PLATFORM	RELEASED	TOTAL UNIT SALES (MILLIONS $)
1	Super Mario Bros.	Platform	NES	1985	40.24
2	Mario Kart Wii	Racing	Wii	2008	34.70
3	New Super Mario Bros.	Platform	DS	2006	29.53
4	New Super Mario Bros. Wii	Platform	Wii	2009	27.58
5	Mario Kart DS	Racing	DS	2005	22.97
6	Super Mario World	Platform	SNES	1990	20.61
7	Super Mario Land	Platform	Game Boy	1989	18.14
8	Super Mario Bros. 3	Platform	NES	1988	17.28
9	Super Mario 64	Platform	NES	1996	11.89
10	Super Mario Land 2: 6 Golden Coins	Platform	Game Boy	1992	11.18

Source: VGChartz

TEAM T-10 REPORT

Party On!

So many of the Mario titles featured here are FANTASTIC party games! Get together with your friends and set up a championship competition to see who has the best jumping, flying and racing skills.

Super Mario World

The original Super Mario World was created for the Super Nintendo Entertainment System (SNES), a console that was made for 13 years between 1990 and 2003.

the lowdown...

SHI

Super Mario 64

When the Nintendo 64 console was released in 1996, this was one of the launch titles. If you have a DS, you may know of Super Mario 64 DS. This remake allowed you to play as Mario, Yoshi and Mario's bro Luigi too.

TOP 10 Coolest Brands

Team T-10 loves it when game designers put a lot of effort into coming up with brilliant-looking brands. These are our favorites.

PLANTS VS. ZOMBIES

After their smart phone gaming success, Plants vs. Zombies has now taken over PS4 and Xbox One consoles with over 2 million unit sales since 2014.

GAME ZONE

Have we left out YOUR favorite game brands? Compile your Top 10 with your friends!

1	Skylanders
2	Super Mario Bros.
3	Plants vs. Zombies
4	LEGO
5	Need For Speed
6	Professor Layton
7	Wii Sports
8	Tony Hawk's Pro Skater
9	Kinect
10	Animal Crossing

Source: VGChartz

LEGO A-GO GO

There have been well over 200 LEGO games released across all of the major platforms, including the 2013 smash hit *LEGO Marvel Super Heroes*.

> WHICH SKYLANDERS ARE THE FAVORITES AMONG YOU AND YOUR FRIENDS? MAKE A TOP 10 LIST!

Skylanders

Since *Skylanders: Spyro's Adventure* in 2011, these interactive figures and games have become a global phenomenon, with nearly 19 million games sold in just four years!

the **lowdown...**

TOP 10 Amazing Character Designs

Some video game characters are just plain OK,
but others have taken genius designing to the next level.

	NAME	GAME(S)
1	Yoshi	Various Nintendo/Mario games
2	Blanka	Street Fighter II
3	HELIX	Darkspore
4	Sackboy	LittleBigPlanet
5	Zero	Warp
6	GlaDOS	Portal 2
7	DeathSpank	DeathSpank
8	Bowser	Various Nintendo/Mario games
9	Sonic the Hedgehog	Various Sega/Sonic games
10	Link	Various Nintendo/Zelda games

Source: VGChartz

SACKBOY IS REALLY A SACKPERSON, AS YOU CAN PLAY AS A SACKGIRL TOO!

MY FAVORITE VIDEO GAME CHARACTER IS JAMES POND IN HIS 1990 ADVENTURE.

Sonic

Sonic the Hedgehog is one of Sega's most successful video game characters. Since he first appeared in 1991, he has been featured in nearly 80 games. Plus, he was in the movie Wreck-it Ralph!

GAME **ZONE**

One of the easiest, quickest and cheapest ways to show a new design idea for a video game is to draw storyboards. Exactly as they sound, these are sketches of how the story and look of the game plays out.

LittleBigPlanet

Actors, writers and all-around treasures Stephen Fry and Hugh Laurie reunite as the voice-over talents in *LittleBigPlanet 3*. They previously starred together in countless comedy TV series and sketches.

the **lowdown...**

Yoshi

He made his video game debut in 1990's *Super Mario World* and has starred in dozens of titles since. Smash hit *Super Mario World 2: Yoshi's Island* has sold more than 7 million copies.

Attack with the L Button.
You don't have to press it repeatedly.

ZONE 4
Ultimate Platforms

Which is your all-time favorite way to play? Let's explore them ALL....

TOP 10 Biggest Selling Gaming Consoles/Platforms

What do you think is the best console? Do your friends have different favorites? Here are the most popular platforms.

	PLATFORM	MADE BY	RELEASED	TOTAL UNIT SALES (MILLIONS)
1	**PlayStation 2**	**Sony**	**2000**	**157.68**
2	Nintendo DS	Nintendo	2004	154.88
3	Game Boy/Game Boy Color	Nintendo	1989 / 1998	118.69
4	PlayStation	Sony	1994	104.25
5	Wii	Nintendo	2006	101.10
6	PlayStation 3	Sony	2006	83.73
7	Xbox 360	Microsoft	2005	83.50
8	Game Boy Advance	Nintendo	2001	81.51
9	PlayStation Portable	Sony	2004	80.82
10	Nintendo Entertainment System	Nintendo	1983	61.91

Source: VGChartz

Touch GO! to play this grid!

ID: 62

Nintendo DS

There's an ongoing fan feud in the video gaming world - "Which is better, the PlayStation or the Xbox?" Well, you might want to know that the tiny, pocket-sized wonder that is the DS has nearly sold the same number of units as the PS3 and the Xbox 360 combined!

PS2

You might have a PS4 or PS3, but the humble PS2 (made between 2000 and 2013) holds the records for the most units sold of its platform (157.68 million) AND its games (1.6 billion)!

the lowdown...

SALES OF THE PS2 SHOT UP TO $250 MILLION ON THE FIRST DAY IT CAME OUT.

GAME BOY

In 1996, two interlinkable games were released for the Game Boy. Those games were the first Pokémon ones... and 87 more releases across all major platforms have followed.

THE WONDER OF Wii

There are more than 101 million Wii owners worldwide. Wii games' sales have generated Nintendo a massive $939 million since the console first launched in 2006.

IF YOU WANT TO GO SUPER-RETRO, FIND THE ORIGINAL 1983 NINTENDO ENTERTAINMENT SYSTEM!

Attack with the L Button. You don't have to press it repeatedly.

ZONE 4: Ultimate Platforms

TOP 10 Coolest Looking Platforms

Over the years of video gaming there have been some truly bizarre-looking consoles. These, however, are all super-awesome.

the lowdown...

3DS

The latest version is the Nintendo 3DS XL. It has an improved 3D graphics display, but the original (pictured) still blows Team T-10's minds. *Pokémon X/Y* remains its best-selling game, selling nearly 13 million copies.

	PLATFORM	MANUFACTURER
1	3DS	Nintendo
2	PS4	Sony
3	SNES	Nintendo
4	PS3	Sony
5	PS Vita	Sony
6	Game Boy	Nintendo
7	Xbox One	Microsoft
8	GameCube	Nintendo
9	Xbox 360	Microsoft
10	Wii	Nintendo

Source: VGChartz

EPIC FACT

The Game Boy was in production for 14 years (1989-2003), selling 118 million units.

Xbox 360

The technology behind the Xbox 360's Kinect system uses special depth sensors, microphones, cameras and even voice-recognition software. No wonder it understands the movement of your body and face!

Top 10 Biggest Selling Home Consoles

If you ever wanted to know what the most popular gaming systems are, wonder no more...

	PLATFORM	MADE BY	RELEASED	TOTAL UNIT SALES (MILLIONS)
1	PlayStation 2	Sony	2000	157.68
2	PlayStation	Sony	1994	104.25
3	Wii	Nintendo	2006	101.10
4	PlayStation 3	Sony	2006	83.73
5	Xbox 360	Microsoft	2005	83.50
6	Nintendo Entertainment System	Nintendo	1983	61.91
7	SNES	Nintendo	1990	49.10
8	N64	Nintendo	1996	32.93
9	Genesis / Megadrive	Sega	1988	29.54
=	Atari 2600	Atari	1977	29.54

Source: VGChartz

Wii

The Wii's controller (known as the Wiimote) can translate the player's arm/body movements into actions with the games! The Wii was Nintendo's follow-up console to the GameCube (which was in production from 2001-07).

PS2 CONTROLLER

The vibrating magic of this controller has been making the gaming experience even cooler since 1997! This, the upgraded DualShock2, first appeared in 2000. Manufacturing stopped in 2013, as DualShock3 & 4 have succeeded it.

EPIC FACT

The PS2 sequel console, the PS3 was the first game platform to use a Blu-ray player as its disc system.

PlayStation Games

ony hold the top 2 spots for oftware sales: the **PS2** has sold n insane 1.6 billion copies, with he **PS** not far behind with 162 million games sold.

DO YOU HAVE AN ALL-TIME FAVORITE VIDEO GAME MEMORY? A FAVORITE LEVEL? WHY NOT WRITE A STORY ABOUT IT!

TOP 10 Biggest Selling Handheld Platforms

Gaming on the go is more popular than ever! Since things got portable, these are the best-sellers...

	HANDHELD PLATFORM	MADE BY	RELEASED	TOTAL UNIT SALES (MILLIONS)
1	Nintendo DS	Nintendo	2004	154.88
2	Game Boy / Game Boy Color	Nintendo	2004	118.69
3	Game Boy Advance	Nintendo	1989 / 1998	81.51
4	PlayStation Portable	Sony	2004	80.82
5	Nintendo 3DS	Nintendo	2011	46.77
6	Game Gear	Sega	1990	10.62
7	PlayStation Vita	Sony	2011	9.07
8	N-Gage	Nokia	2003	3
9	Neo Geo Pocket/Pocket Color	SNK	1998/1999	2
10	TurboExpress	NEC	1990	1.5

Source: VGChartz

WHAT IS THE HIGHEST SCORE YOU'VE EVER ACHIEVED ON YOUR FAVORITE GAME? ASK YOUR FRIENDS FOR THEIRS TOO.

the **lowdown**...

DS

One of the most popular series for the DS is the Brain Age training games. All ages - even moms and dads - enjoy them, which explains why 35 million have been bought since their 2005 debut.

PS VITA

This flashier and faster successor to Sony's popular PSP (PlayStation Portable) first appeared in stores in 2011. The PSV can even receive games from the PS4 so they can be played remotely.

TOP 10 Platforms with the Most Games

With the video game industry stronger than ever, let's take a closer look at exactly how many of the pixelated adventures have been created for the most successful systems...

OVER 800 MILLION UNITS OF GAMES HAVE BEEN SOLD FOR THE NINTENDO DS!

GAME ZONE

Can you think of a game that you play with your friends that ISN'T a video game? Could it be developed into a cool game idea? Start brainstorming!

	PLATFORM	MADE BY	YEAR RELEASED	TOTAL GAMES MADE
1	**PC**	**Microsoft**	**1982**	**9,036**
2	Nintendo DS	Nintendo	2004	3,994
3	XBox 360	Microsoft	2005	3,612
4	PS2	Sony	2000	3,549
5	PS3	Sony	2006	3,182
6	Wii	Nintendo	2006	2,792
7	Playstation	Sony	1994	2,680
8	PSP	Sony	2004	1,802
9	Game Boy Advance	Nintendo	2001	1,690
10	Game Boy / Game Boy Color	Nintendo	1989/1998	1,602

Source: VGChartz

EPIC FACT

More than 52 million units of the DS have been sold worldwide.

Game Boy Advance

Fondly known among gamers as the GBA, this model came just before the Nintendo DS. It was produced for eight years until 2008.

the **lowdown...**

DS

With nearly 155 million people tapping away on Nintendo DS since its 2004 release, it's clear who dominates the portable gaming market. Sony's PSV has almost 10 million sales, and even the PSP only notches up around 80 million.

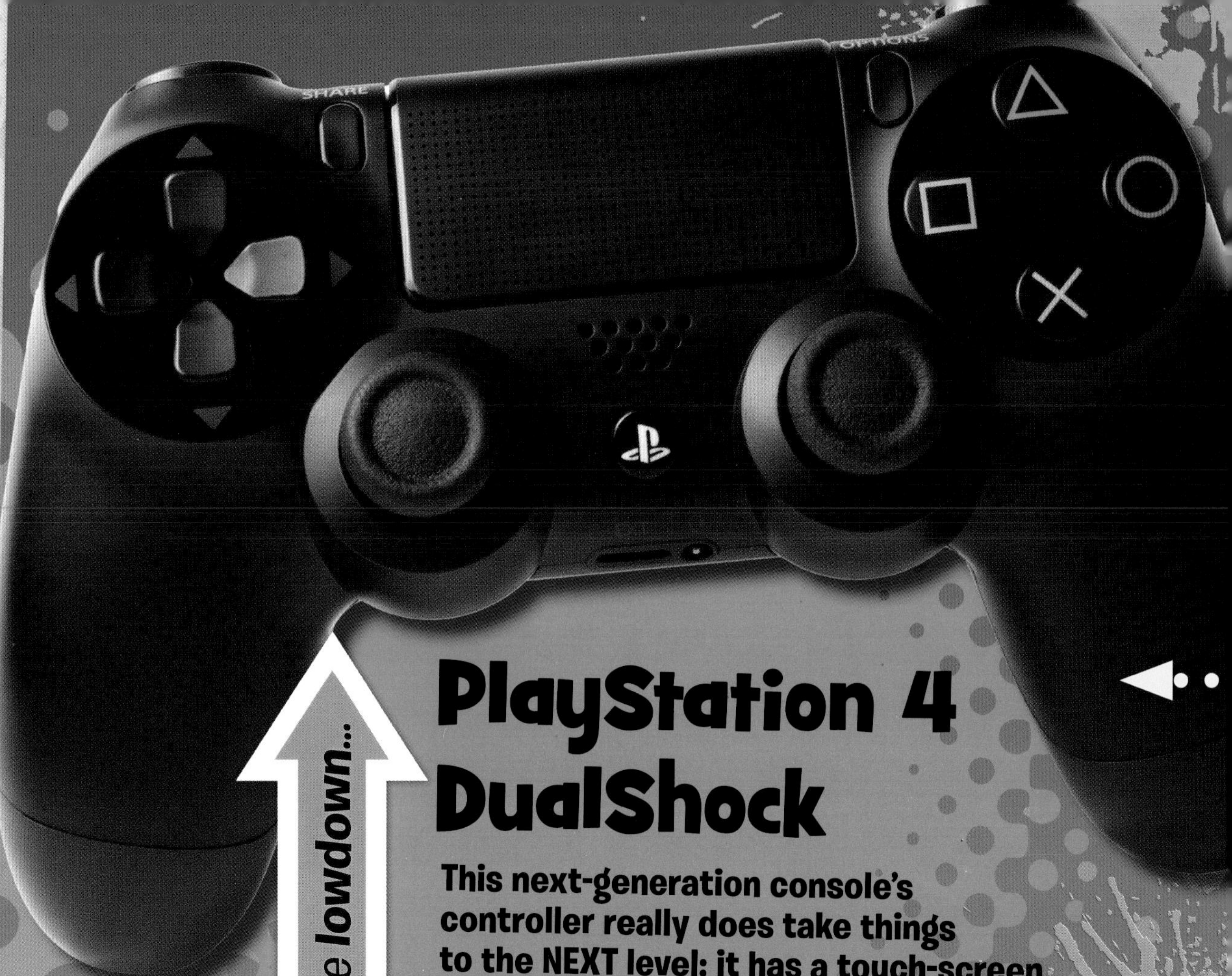

the lowdown...

PlayStation 4 DualShock

This next-generation console's controller really does take things to the NEXT level: it has a touch-screen AND headphone socket for even more exciting gameplay.

GAME ZONE

The PS4 DualShock 4 has only been around since November 2013.

NINTENDO GAMECUBE

TOP 10 Amazing Controllers

As the years have gone by, it seems that manufacturers have wanted us to get used to using more and more buttons to jump, smash and steer our way around their game worlds...

	CONTROLLER	YEAR RELEASED	TOTAL BUTTONS
1	PlayStation 4 DualShock 4	2013	17
=	PlayStation 3 DualShock 3 Sixaxis	2007	17
=	PlayStation 2 DualShock 2	2000	17
=	PlayStation Dual Analog	1997	17
5	GameCube Wavebird	2002	14
=	Xbox 360	2005	14
7	Wii U	2012	13
=	Xbox One	2013	13
9	Dreamcast controller and VMU	1998	12
10	N64	1996	11

Source: VGChartz

HOW MANY OF THESE AWESOME CONTROLLERS HAVE YOU PLAYED WITH? CAN YOU THINK OF AN EVEN BETTER DESIGN? GET SKETCHING!

Wavebird

This bizarre, spaceship-type controller was released with the GameCube, Nintendo's console that was in production from 2001-2007. Like modern controllers, it was wireless too.

ZONE 5

Beyond the Game

Video games now dominate the big screen as well as the small one....

THE DIRECTOR OF WRECK-IT RALPH ALSO WORKED ON FUTURAMA AND THE SIMPSONS.

the **lowdown**...

Wreck-it Ralph

The cast who provided the voices for the characters in *Wreck-it Ralph* included: John C. Reilly (Ralph), who also starred in *Guardians of the Galaxy*, plus Sarah Silverman (Vanellope) who turned up in *The Muppets* movie!

EPIC FACT

Disney have wanted to make an animated movie about games for over 30 years! Fix-it Felix was originally going to be the star.

TOP 10 Biggest Movies About Video Gaming

The movie world has come up with a lot of original stories based around the concept of video games...

	MOVIE	RELEASED	BOX OFFICE (US$)
1	**Wreck-it Ralph**	**2012**	**471,222,889**
2	Tron Legacy	2010	400,062,763
3	Spy Kids 3D: Game Over	2003	197,011,982
4	War Games	1983	79,567,667
5	Scott Pilgrim vs. The World	2010	47,664,559
6	Tron	1982	33,000,000
7	The Last Starfighter	1984	28,733,290
8	Stay Alive	2006	27,105,095
9	The Wizard	1989	14,278,900
10	Cloak & Dagger	1984	9,719,952

Source: IMDB.com

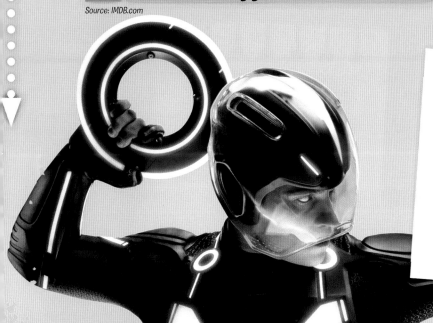

Tron Legacy

Believe it or not, Tron Legacy was a direct sequel to the original Disney movie that came out 28 years before it! Plus, Daft Punk provided music for the sequel AND made an appearance in the film.

Biggest Video Game Movie Adaptations

TOP 10

How many of these movie adaptations have you seen? These 10 cover a LOT of different gaming genres...

	MOVIE	RELEASED	BASED ON GAME/ FRANCHISE	BOX OFFICE (US$)
1	**Prince of Persia: Sands of Time**	**2010**	**Prince of Persia**	**336,365,67**
2	**Lara Croft: Tomb Raider**	2001	Tomb Raider	274,703,340
3	**Need For Speed**	2014	Need for Speed	203,277,636
4	**Pokémon: The First Movie**	1998	Pokémon	163,644,662
5	**Lara Croft Tomb Raider: The Cradle of Life**	2003	Tomb Raider	156,505,388
6	**Pokémon: The Movie 2000**	1999	Pokémon	133,949,270
7	**Mortal Kombat**	1995	Mortal Kombat	122,195,920
8	**Street Fighter**	1994	Street Fighter	99,423,521
9	**Max Payne**	2008	Max Payne	85,416,905
10	**Final Fantasy: The Spirits Within**	2001	Final Fantasy	85,131,830

Source: IMDB.com

TOMB RAIDER

With over 36 million games sold worldwide, it's no surprise Lara Croft became the star of two hit movies. The first, the more popular of the two, got lead actress Angelina Jolie a Saturn Award nomination for Best Actress in 2002.

Prince of Persia

This big-screen version of the *Prince of Persia* game series was SO action-packed that it scored a nomination at the World Stunt Awards in 2011!

Gemma Power

Prince of Persia actress Gemma Arterton also starred in the 2008 James Bond adventure *Quantum of Solace*.

PRINCE OF PERSIA STAR JAKE GYLLENHAAL HAS BEEN IN OVER 30 FILMS SINCE HIS 1991 DEBUT IN CITY SLICKERS WHEN HE WAS JUST 11 YEARS OLD.

EPIC FACT

Since the first *Prince of Persia* game was released in 1989, the puzzle-adventure series has scooped over 13 million unit sales worldwide.

Angelina Jolie

Angelia Jolie played adventurer Lara Croft in the movies, but she's also a hugely successful film director and producer too. She's had over 85 award nominations and over 40 award wins.

the *lowdown...*

EPICFACT

Jolie starred in two big screen adventures as Lara Croft, released in 2001 and 2003. They took in a total of more than $430 million around the world.

SEQUEL POWER

Tomb Raider II, released for the PS2 back in 1997 remains the most successful Lara Croft game ever, with more than 5 million copies sold.

TOP 10 Coolest Casting of Gaming Characters in Movies

These actors could not have been more perfectly cast...

	ACTOR	CHARACTER PLAYED	FILM ADAPTION OF GAME	YEAR
1	Angelina Jolie	Lara Croft	Tomb Raider movies	2001-3
2	Aaron Paul	Tobey Marshall	Need for Speed	2014
3	Mila Kunis	Mona Sax	Max Payne	2008
4	Kristin Kreuk	Chun-Lee	Street Fighter: The Legend of Chun-Li	2009
5	Anna Torv (voice)	Nariko	Heavenly Sword	2014
6	Jake Gyllenhaal	Prince Dastan	Prince of Persia: The Sands of Time	2010
7	Kylie Minogue	Cammy	Street Fighter	1994
8	Jason Statham	Farmer	In the Name of the King: A Dungeon Siege Tale	2006
9	Bob Hoskins	Super Mario	Super Mario Bros.	1993
10	Scott Wolf	Billy Lee	Double Dragon	1994

Source: IMDB.com

ANNA TORV WON A SATURN AWARD FOR BEST ACTRESS THREE YEARS IN A ROW FOR HER ROLE ON FRINGE.

Aaron Paul

This actor, the star of the *Need for Speed* movie has been in the business since 1998. His car-racing hit film more than tripled its budget cost and made more than $200 million.

Longest Running TV Shows Based on Gaming

You read that right. There have been LOADS of TV shows about video games!

	TV SHOW	BASED ON GAME FRANCHISE	YEARS ON AIR	TOTAL EPISODES
1	Pokémon	Pokémon	19 (1997-present)	900+
2	Digimon	Digimon	12 (1999-2011)	332
3	Kirby: Right Back at Ya	Kirby	2 (2001-03)	100
4	Saturday Supercade	Various	2 (1983-85)	97
5	Sonic X	Sonic the Hedgehog	2 (2003-05)	78
6	Mega Man Star Force	Mega Man	2 (2006-08)	76
7	Monster Rancher	Monster Rancher	2 (1999-2001)	73
8	Adventures of Sonic the Hedgehog	Sonic the Hedgehog	3 (1993-96)	67
9	The Super Mario Bros. Super Show!	Super Mario Bros.	1 (1989)	65
10	Bomberman Jetters	Bomberman	1 (2002-03)	52

Source: IMDB.com

EPIC FACT

You can fight as Pikachu in the Super Smash Bros. game series too.

Pokémon

Eighteen seasons after its 1997 TV debut, the power Pokémon continues. Aside from the 900 episodes, there have been a further 37 specials AND 18 movie

HOW DO YOU FIT 3,000 PIKACHUS ON A BUS? POKE 'EM ON!

the lowdown...

Sonic

With his first game launched in 1991, the loveable blue hedgehog has sold over 100 million copies of his games. He's also had his own TV series and comic, and he appeared in Disney's *Wreck-It Ralph*.

TEAM T-10 REPORT

To put into perspective how popular and successful the Pokémon TV series is, let's compare it to one of the biggest animated shows in the world. *The Simpsons* has aired 567 episodes since its 1989 debut, which means Pokémon has made almost double the number in half the time!

TOP 10

Coolest Collector's Edition Extras

Team T-10 loves to get Special Editions, and these are our 10 all-time favorites...

Dragon Power

This incredible edition come with two exclusive Frieza Soldier's Battle Suits. Super Saiyan 4 Vegeta as a playable character, a huge Trunk Master Stars Piece figurine AND an amazing steelbook case. Sweet!

THE BEATLES ROCK BAND GAME ISN'T MANUFACTURED ANY MORE, SO YOU'LL NEED TO SEEK OUT SECOND-HAND OR UNSOLD COPIES IF YOU WANT THIS AWESOME GAME.

	EXTRAS/MERCHANDISE	FROM
1	**Steelbook, pin badge, poster**	The Legend of Zelda: Majora's Mask 3D Special Edition
2	**Drippy plush toy & Wizard's Companion Book**	Ni No Kuni: The Wrath of the White Witch – Wizard's Edition
3	**Replicas of The Beatles' instruments**	The Beatles Rock Band Limited Edition
4	**Trunks Master Stars Piece figure**	Dragon Ball Xenoverse: Trunks' Travel Edition
5	**Exclusive laser cell artwork**	Naruto Shippuden: Ultimate Ninja Storm 2
6	**Cloth map, DVD, soundtrack, manual**	World of Warcraft: Ultimate Experience
7	**Figurines of Link & Phantom Zelda**	The Legend of Zelda: Spirit Tracks
8	**History of Mario book, soundtrack**	Super Mario All-Stars 25th Anniversary Edition
9	**Carry case, premium turntables**	DJ Hero: Renegade Edition
10	**Gold ring, documentary, lenticular design**	Sonic Generations

Source: IMDB.com

the lowdown...

DJ HERO

Five million copies of DJ Hero games have been sold, with this, the first version, remaining the most popular. It was created as a side-step from the success of party game series *Guitar Hero*. More than 100 songs were featured in its mixes.

First Ever Animated Movies Based on Video Games

You may have seen the likes of the *Prince of Persia* movie, but big screen versions began with animated epics...

EPIC FACT

Fan-favorite Chun-Li was the first ever female character to be introduced into the Street Fighter game series back in 1991.

Street Fighter II

Street Fighter is the most influential fighting game ever, with dozens of imitators. Capcom's classic combat game has had success on every platform. It's still their most successful game series of all time, with 32 million copies sold.

the lowdown...

	MOVIE	BASED ON GAME FRANCHISE	DATE RELEASED
1	Super Mario Bros.: The Great Mission to Rescue Princess Peach!	Super Mario Bros.	July 20, 1986
2	Fatal Fury: The Motion Picture	Fatal Fury	July 16, 1994
3	Street Fighter II: The Animated Movie	Street Fighter II	Aug. 8, 1994
4	Pokémon: The First Movie	Pokémon	July 18, 1998
5	Pokémon: The Movie 2000	Pokémon	July 17, 1999
6	Pokémon 3: The Movie	Pokémon	July 8, 2000
7	Pokémon 4Ever	Pokémon	July 7, 2001
8	Pokémon Heroes: Latios and Latias	Pokémon	July 13, 2002
9	Pokémon: Jirachi Wish Maker	Pokémon	July 19, 2003
10	Pokémon: Destiny Deoxys	Pokémon	July 17, 2004

Source: IMDB.com

First Movie

As if the Pokémon franchise wasn't powerful enough, the debut movie took in more than $163 million at box offices around the world. It cost $30 million to make, so it made more than five times its budget.

Ten thousand people attend PLAY: The Games Festival each year. It also features collectible card games and board games.

IS THERE A VIDEO GAMES CONVENTION NEAR WHERE YOU LIVE? CHECK WITH YOUR FAMILY AND FRIENDS, AND MAYBE YOU CAN PLAN A TRIP!

the lowdown...

Dragon Con

One of the most popular conventions in the U.S., Dragon Con runs for four days. It now attracts nearly 60,000 people every year.

Super Trooper

Conventions mean cosplay (costume-play)! Fans and professional actors turn up in amazingly accurate versions of movie, TV and video game characters.

TOP 10 Biggest Gaming Conventions

These days, pop culture conventions are more popular than ever. TV shows, movies, comics and even video games draw crowds of thousands...

	CONVENTION	LOCATION	YEAR BEGAN	TOTAL YEARS
1	**CoastCon**	**Mississippi**	**1977**	**38**
2	PLAY: The Games Festival	Modena, Italy	1982	33
=	I-CON	New York	1982	33
=	MidSouthCon	Tennessee	1982	33
5	BASHCon	Ohio	1985	30
=	Genericon	New York	1985	30
7	Dragon Con	Georgia	1987	28
8	U-Con	Michigan	1988	27
9	DemiCon	Iowa	1990	25

Source: VGChartz

MidSouthCon

Although one of the smaller conventions, Memphis' MidSouthCon has a dedicated fan-base who return annually. Their special guests have included sci-fi writer Kevin J. Anderson.

TIME TO GET INTERACTIVE!

It's almost time to say farewell to the fantastic gaming characters and worlds we've met on this T-10 trip. Before we go, test your knowledge of them with this quiz....

Questions from... ZONE 1

1 Can you remember which is the biggest selling console game of all time?

2 Who is the star of *LEGO City*?

A: Pacey McSheen

B: Chase McCain

C: Blaze McCayne

3 Which has sold more copies on the PS4, *FIFA 15* or *NBA 2K15*?

Questions from... ZONE 2

2 True or false: LEGO video games have sold over 108 million units?

TRUE   FALSE

1 Can you put these genres in the order of how popular they are?

A: Puzzle

B: Platform

C: Sports

3 Which game are these characters from?

A

B

C

Questions from... ZONE 3

1 What is the name of this Space T-rex/Dinobot?

A: Sludge

B: Grimlock

C: Jaws

2 What year did *Super Mario Bros.* (the biggest Mario game ever) come out?

3 Double challenge: who is this, and which game did he first appear in?

Questions from... ZONE 4

1 Can you name two controllers that have exactly 13 buttons each?

2 True or false: the Nintendo Game Boy is the biggest selling handheld console ever.

3 Which of these has sold more copies: PSV (PlayStation Vita) or PSP (PlayStation Portable)?

Questions from... ZONE 5

1 Who is this? She played Lara Croft twice in movie adaptations.

2 Since 1997, have there been more than 900 or 9,000 episodes of the Pokémon TV series?

900

9,000

3 Can you put these video game movie adaptations in the order of their box office success?

A: *Street Fighter*

B: *Prince of Persia: Sands of Time*

C: *Need for Speed*

ANSWERS:

ZONE 5
1: Angelina Jolie
2: 900
3: B, C, A

ZONE 4
1: Wii and Xbox One's controllers
2: FALSE: it's the Nintendo DS
3: PSP

ZONE 3
1: B
2: 1985
3: Yoshi, who debuted in *Super Mario World* (1990)

ZONE 2
1: C, B, A
2: TRUE
3: Pokémon Black/White Version

ZONE 1
1: *Wii Sports*
2: B
3: *FIFA 15*

Also available:

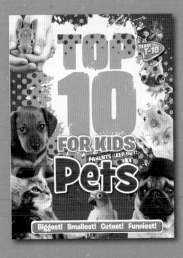
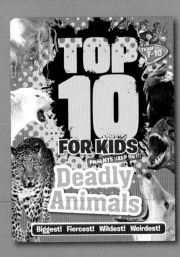

PICTURE CREDITS

The publishers would like to acknowledge the following sources in the book:

4. Pop Cap Games (Plants v Zombies), Nintendo (Mario), Warner Bros. Interactive Entertainment (LEGO Batman), Mojang (Minecraft), SCEE (Ratchet), 5. Nintendo (Yoshi), SCEE (Sackboy), Activision (Skylanders), 8. SCEE (Ratchet), EA (FIFA15), Nintendo (Mario & Lego City Undercover), Ubisoft (Just Dance), 9. EA (FIFA13 & Madden NFL 15), Mark Collinson/Alamy, 10. Karl Gehring/The Denver Post via Getty Images (Tetris), 10-11. Barone Firenze/Shutterstock.com, 11. Maurice Crooks/Alamy (Wii Golf), 12. Nintendo (Lego City Undercover & Pikmin 3), 13. Akio Kon/Bloomberg via Getty Images, 14. Nintendo (Wii Sports), Manaemedia/Shutterstock.com, 15. Nintendo (Mario), Ubisoft (Just Dance), 16. EA (FIFA 13), 16-17. SSCE (Gran Turismo), 18. EA (Madden NFL 15), 18-19. EA (FIFA15), 20-21. EA (Need for Speed), 22. SCEE (Gravity Rush), 23. EA (Need for Speed), SCEE (Little Big Planet), 24. Microsoft Game Studios (Forza Motorsport), 25. EA (FIFA12), Microsoft Game Studios (Kinect Adventures), 26-27. Nintendo (Super Mario 3D, Animal Crossing), 28. ArcadeImages/Alamy (Pac-Man), 28-29. Capcom (Street Fighter II), 29. Kevin Britland/Alamy (Donkey Kong), 30. David Lichtneker/Alamy, 30-31. SCEE (Ratchet), 32. iStockphoto.com (PS3), DPA Picture Alliance Archive/Alamy (Kinect), 33. Lightly Salted/Alamy (Wii), Mark Collinson/Alamy (Kinect), 34. Warner Bros. Interactive Entertainment (LEGO Batman), Blizzard Entertainment (World of Warcraft), 34-35. Mojang (Minecraft), Nintendo (Mario), SSCE (Gran Turismo), 36-37. Nintendo (Mario & Super Smash Bros.), 38-39 & 39. EA (FIFA14), 39 Nintendo/Sega (Mario & Sonic), 40-41. Nintendo (Super Mario), 42. Blizzard Entertainment (World of Warcraft), Nintendo/The Pokémon Company (Black & White), 44. Warner Bros. Interactive Entertainment (LEGO Batman), 45. Mojang (Minecraft), 46. Nintendo (Mario), 46-47. EA (Gran Turismo), 48. Activision (Skylanders), Pop Cap Games (Plants v Zombies), Nintendo (Yoshi), EA (NFS: Most Wanted), SCEE (Little Big Planet), 49. Activision (Transformers), Pop Cap Games (Plants v Zombies), 50. SCEE/WB Games/AsiaSoft (DC Universe), 50-51. Moviestore Collection/Rex (Final Fantasy), 51. Istock.com (The Incredibles), 52. Ethan Miller/Getty Images, 52-53. EA (NFS: Most Wanted), 53. Photofusion/Rex, 54. Namco Bandai (Ni No Kuni), 54-55. Activision (Transformers), 56. Nintendo (Mario), 58. Pop Cap Games (Plants v Zombies), 58-59. Activision (Skylanders), 60. Nintendo (Sonic), 61. SCEE (Little Big Planet), Nintendo (Yoshi), 62. Mouse in the House/Alamy (PS3), Hugh Threlfall/Alamy (controller), Thinkstock.com (DS), 63. Thinkstock.com (Gameboy), Vangelis Vassalakis/Alamy (Gameboy Advance), Istockphoto.com (PS Vita), 64. Realimage/Alamy (Nintendo DS), 65. Mouse in the House/Alamy (PS3), Thinkstock.com (Gameboy), 66. Shutterstock.com (Wii), Thinkstock.com (3DS), 67. Istockphoto.com, 68. Thinkstock.com, 69. Hugh Threlfall/Alamy (PS2 controller), Art Directors & TRIP/Alamy (games), 71. Hugh Threlfall/Alamy (Nintendo DS), Istockphoto.com (PS Vita), 72. Cornerstone Photos/Alamy, 73. Vangelis Vassalakis/Alamy (Gameboy Advance), 74. Thinkstock.com (Playstation controller), Evan-Amos (GameCube), 76. Photo 12/Alamy (Wreck-It Ralph), Walt Disney-Pictures/The Kobal Collection (Prince of Persia), Courtesy Everett Collection/Rex (Street Fighter II), DIC Enterprises/SEGA/Reteitalia/Telecino/The Kobal Collection (Sonic), Walt Disney Pictures/The Kobal Collection (Tron Legacy), 77. Bandai Namco Games (Dragon Ball), Paramount/The Kobal Collection (Tomb Raider), 78. Photo 12/Alamy. 79. Walt Disney Pictures/The Kobal Collection, 80. Paramount/The Kobal Collection, 81. Walt Disney-Pictures/The Kobal Collection, 82. Paramount/The Kobal Collection (Tomb Raider), DFree/Shutterstock.com, 83. Featureflash/Shutterstock.com, 84. Nintendo/OLM/Summit Media/TV Tokyo/The Kobal Collection, 85. DIC Enterprises/SEGA/Reteitalia/Telecino/The Kobal Collection, 86. Bandai Namco Games (Dragon Ball), 87. Activision (DJ Hero), 88. Courtesy Everett Collection/Rex, 89. Pikachu Projects '98/The Kobal Collection, 90. Tish Wells/MCT/MCT via Getty Images, 90-91. Erik S. Lesser/epa/Corbis, 91. The Commercial Appeal/Corbis, 92. Pop Cap Games (Plants v Zombies), SCEE (Little Big Planet), Activision (Transformers), Mojang (Minecraft), 93. Warner Bros. Interactive Entertainment (LEGO Batman), Nintendo (Mario & Yoshi), Activision (Skylanders), EA (Need for Speed)

ACKNOWLEDGMENTS

Top 10 Parents Keep Out! Pets Produced by SHUBROOK BROS. CREATIVE and WildPixel Ltd.

Writer & Researcher: Paul Terry

Illustrations: Huw J

Picture Research: SpookyFish

Special thanks to...

Ian Turp & Marc Glanville at Getty Images

David Martill, Palaeobiologist